GROUP
BIBLE STUDY

# HOLY SPIRIT:
## Come, Holy Spirit

## by Lyman Coleman

A Serendipity House resource published by
ABINGDON/Nashville, Tennessee 37202

ISBN 0-687-37321-2

*"I am telling you the truth: whoever
believes in me will do what I do—yes,
he will do even greater things."*
John 14:12, GNB

**You're invited
to feast
at God's table.**

**The Holy Spirit
is your host.
Eat
and be filled.
Drink
and be satisfied.**

**Let your soul
delight
in God's greatness.**

**RSVP**

**Call collect!**

**Don't delay.**

# Seasons of the Soul

Before you start on this course, take a moment and check where you are right now in your spiritual life. Compare your life to the four seasons of nature:

- ☐ **SPRING:** turning the soil, planting the seed
- ☐ **SUMMER:** rapid growth, fruit-bearing
- ☐ **FALL:** harvest, separating wheat/chaff
- ☐ **WINTER:** letting the ground lie fallow/rest

All four seasons are essential for spiritual abundance. And you may be in a different season for the different areas of your life. Check the season below that symbolizes where you are in each area.

Then, at the close of the course, check your spiritual life again to see how your spiritual life has changed during the course.

**BEFORE**                                                                                       **AFTER**

| SPRING | SUMMER | FALL | WINTER | | SPRING | SUMMER | FALL | WINTER |
|---|---|---|---|---|---|---|---|---|
| ☐ | ☐ | ☐ | ☐ | In my desire to worship God for who he is … | ☐ | ☐ | ☐ | ☐ |
| ☐ | ☐ | ☐ | ☐ | In my understanding of God's purpose for my life … | ☐ | ☐ | ☐ | ☐ |
| ☐ | ☐ | ☐ | ☐ | In my devotional/prayer life … | ☐ | ☐ | ☐ | ☐ |
| ☐ | ☐ | ☐ | ☐ | In being involved in a life-enhancing fellowship … | ☐ | ☐ | ☐ | ☐ |
| ☐ | ☐ | ☐ | ☐ | In my understanding of the deeper things of the Spirit … | ☐ | ☐ | ☐ | ☐ |
| ☐ | ☐ | ☐ | ☐ | In responding to God's leading in daily discipleship … | ☐ | ☐ | ☐ | ☐ |

# Invitation

*(Instructions in Leader's Guide)*

## PRELIMINARY EXERCISE

### Memories

Get acquainted with someone (that you do not know very well) by sharing some of the significant people in your life.—LEFT COLUMN.

Then, take your partner; get together with two others and share your concept of the Holy Spirit—RIGHT COLUMN.

## GROUPS OF 2

1. The person who made me feel special when I was a child was. . . .
2. The person who took time out to play with me as a child was. . . .
3. The person I went to for comfort as a child was. . . .
4. The person who encouraged me to think about God was. . . .
5. The person who stood by me when I blew it was. . . .
6. The person who helped me to see my potential in Christ was. . . .

## GROUPS OF 4

When I think of the Holy Spirit, I think of:
(circle one in each line)

close friend . . . . . . . . . . . . . . . distant relative

something mysterious . . . . . . . . . . . . . . . . . . . . something wonderful

a million years ago . . . . . . . . . . . . . . . . . today

deep flowing river . . . . . . . bubbling fountain

mighty wind . . . . . . . . . . . . . . . . gentle breeze

glowing candle . . . . . . . . . . . . . . blast furnace

rocking chair . . . . . . . . . . . . . . . . . . . . . hot seat

> Jesus said . . . "There was once a man who was giving a great feast to which he invited many people. When it was time for the feast, he sent his servant to tell his guests, 'Come, everything is ready!' But they all began, one after another, to make excuses. The first one told the servant, 'I have bought a field and must go and look at it; please accept my apologies.' Another one said, 'I have bought five pairs of oxen and am on my way to try them out; please accept my apologies.' Another one said, 'I have just gotten married, and for that reason I cannot come.' The servant went back and told all this to his master. The master was furious and said to his servant, 'Hurry out to the streets and alleys of the town, and bring back the poor, the crippled, the blind, and the lame.' Soon the servant said, 'Your order has been carried out, sir, but there is room for more.' So the master said to the servant, 'Go out to the country roads and lanes and make people come in, so that my house will be full. I tell you all that none of those men who were invited will taste my dinner.' "  *Luke 14:16-24, GNB*

This story was told by Jesus while he was eating a meal at the home of one of the leading Pharisees and a dispute arose over healing a cripple on the Sabbath.

# RELATIONAL BIBLE STUDY

## An Offer You Can't Refuse

Where are you right now in your spiritual life? Try to find yourself in the Scripture story and complete the questionnaire about your own spiritual life.

**RESEARCH:**

1. **What do you feel is the main point of this Scripture story?**
   a. **The determination of the MAN who offered the "great feast"**
   b. **The difficulty that the SERVANT had in getting the special guests to come**
   c. **The insulting behavior of the SPECIAL GUESTS by making excuses**
   d. **The response of the POOR, CRIPPLED, BLIND, and LAME to the invitation**

2. **What is the "great feast" referring to in this Scripture story?**
   a. **The abundance of God**
   b. **Citizenship in the new kingdom that Christ announced**
   c. **A spiritual new birth**
   d. **A party for losers who want to be winners**
   e. **The wedding banquet of Christ and his bride, the "church"**

3. **Who are the people in this Scripture story?**

   **The MAN is:**

   **The SERVANT is:**

   **The SPECIAL GUESTS are:**

   **The POOR, CRIPPLED, BLIND, and LAME are:**

**MY OWN STORY:** Read over the Scripture again and respond to the questions about your own spiritual experience.

1. **Spiritually, the first time I can recall feeling God's invitation to his "great feast" was:**
   a. **When I was a child**
   b. **Many years ago**
   c. **Recently**
   d. **What call? My phone hasn't rung yet**
   e. **I'm waiting for a call—that's why I'm here**

2. **When it comes to deeper spiritual things, my response to God's invitation is best summarized:**
   a. **I'll be there, but I'm on a diet**
   b. **I'll have to talk it over with my friends first**
   c. **I'll be there, but I'll have to leave before the orchestra starts**
   d. **Can I bring my own Big Mac?**
   e. **I'll be there with bells on**
   f. **I'll come if I can bring my friends**
   g. **I have some mental reservations about the invitation**
   h. **Give me a day to think about it**

3. **The spiritual diet that I have been living on lately has been mainly:** (circle two)
   a. **Baby food**
   b. **TV dinners**
   c. **Meat and potatoes**
   d. **Dehydrated food**
   e. **Generic (no brand name) food**
   f. **Junk food**
   g. **Canned goods**
   h. **Pure organic food**
   i. **Gourmet feast**
   j. **Bread and wine**

4. **The reason why I signed up for this course was:**
   a. **To find out what God's "great feast" is all about**
   b. **To find out if there is something more to the "feast" than I am experiencing**
   c. **To change my diet**
   d. **To get to know others at the banquet table**
   e. **Stop eating my meals all alone**
   f. **Ask me tomorrow**

# DEEPER BIBLE STUDY

## About Me ... and God's Riches in Christ

Get in touch with how you feel about your spiritual life in the poem below. Then, dialogue with God through the Scripture about your hopes and dreams for this course.

### Something More

God, there's got to be more
    to life
    than what I'm experiencing!
More to church ... than sitting.
More to creeds ... than repetition.
More to prayer ... than pleading.
More to love ... than feelings.
More to life ... than existing.
More to friends ... than learning.

Tell me, God ... there IS something more.

The last time I felt like this poem was....

Right now, the something more I need in my life is....

## REFLECTION

1. God, I have lived so long on junk food that I don't know how I would feel at your banquet. Are you sure that this feast is for me? That is, do you think that I would fit in?

*The Lord says,*
    *"Come, everyone who is thirsty—*
        *here is water!*
    *Come, you that have no money—*
        *buy grain and eat!*
    *Come! Buy wine and milk—*
        *it will cost you nothing!*

*Why spend money on what does not satisfy?*
    *Why spend your wages and still be hungry?*
*Listen to me and do what I say,*
    *and you will enjoy the best food of all."*

*Isaiah 55:1-2, GNB*

The words here that really speak to me are....

2. If all this is true, how come I feel as I do right now? What is it going to take to make me see the "feast" as it really is?

*I ask that your minds may be opened to see his light, so that you will know what is the hope to which he has called you, how rich are the wonderful blessings he promises his people, and how very great is his power at work in us who believe.*    *Ephesians 1:18-19, GNB*

The thing that is really keeping me from getting in on this feast is....

## SELF-EXAMINATION

Here is the spiritual "great feast" that is rightfully yours as part of God's family through Jesus Christ. Read over the things that Jesus Christ accomplished for you and indicate your response to each item by putting a dot on the line—somewhere in between HO HUM and HALLELUJAH! For instance, on the first item, you might put the dot midway between the two extremes because this fact makes you feel good ... but not really excited.

Ho Hum       Hallelujah!

**I AM A PARTAKER OF GOD'S GRACE:** In Christ,
I have been chosen to receive the free gift of God.
_________________________

> *But God, who is rich in mercy, out of the great love with which he loved us, even when
> we were dead through our trespasses, made us alive together with Christ (by grace
> you have been saved), and raised us up with him, and made us sit with him in
> heavenly places in Christ Jesus.*        *Ephesians 2:4-6, RSV*

**I AM REDEEMED:** In Christ, I have been released from the
prison house of sin. My freedom was purchased by Christ's
payment for my sin.
_________________________

> *In him [Christ] we have redemption through his blood, the forgiveness of our
> trespasses.*        *Ephesians 1:7, RSV*

**I AM RECONCILED:** In Christ, my broken relationship with
God has been restored. The "bridge over troubled waters" is
Jesus Christ himself.
_________________________

> *All this is from God, who through Christ reconciled us to himself and gave us the
> ministry of reconciliation.*        *2 Corinthians 5:18-19, RSV*

**I AM FORGIVEN:** In Christ, the debt for my sins has been
"paid in full." Jesus Christ secured my release from "death
row" by his own death.
_________________________

> *And you, who were dead in trespasses ... God made alive together with him, having
> forgiven us all our trespasses.*        *Colossians 2:13, RSV*

**I AM ADOPTED:** In Christ, I have been legally taken into the
family of God as a joint-heir with Christ.
_________________________

> *He [God] destined us in love to be his sons through Jesus Christ, according to the
> purpose of his will.*        *Ephesians 1:5, RSV*

**I AM JUSTIFIED:** In Christ, I have been declared okay, just as
though I'd never sinned.
_________________________

> *Therefore, since we are justified by faith, we have peace with God, through our Lord
> Jesus Christ.*        *Romans 5:1, RSV*

**I AM A CITIZEN OF HEAVEN:** In Christ, I have been given a
new citizenship, a new world and a new allegiance.
_________________________

> *So then you are no longer strangers and sojourners, but you are fellow citizens with
> the saints and members of the household of God.*        *Ephesians 2:19, RSV*

**I AM A ROYAL PRIEST:** In Christ, I am allowed direct access
to God.
_________________________

> *But you are a chosen race, a royal priesthood, a holy nation, God's own people, that
> you may declare the wonderful deeds of him who called you out of darkness into his
> marvelous light.*        *1 Peter 2:9, RSV*


## APPLICATION

Take a few minutes and "feast" on the Scripture below—the vision of the throne room of heaven
described in Revelation. The Scripture begins with a song that the angels are singing to Jesus
Christ for what he has accomplished on earth. Let the Spirit direct your thoughts into a time of
prayer, based on the Scripture.

> *And they [the angels] sang a new song, saying,*
> > *"Worthy art thou [Jesus Christ] to take the scroll and to open its seals,*
> > *for thou wast slain and by thy blood didst ransom men for God*
> > *from every tribe and tongue and people and nation,*
> > *and hast made them a kingdom and priests to our God,*
> > *and they shall reign on earth."*
>
> *Then I looked, and I heard around the throne and the living creatures and the elders the
> voice of many angels, numbering myriads of myriads and thousands of thousands, saying
> with a loud voice, "Worthy is the Lamb who was slain, to receive power and wealth and
> wisdom and might and honor and glory and blessing!" And I heard every creature in
> heaven and on earth and under the earth and in the sea, and all therein, saying, "To him
> who sits upon the throne and to the Lamb be blessing and honor and glory and might for
> ever and ever!"*        *Revelation 5:9-13, RSV*

# Overflowing

*(Instructions in Leader's Guide)*

## PRELIMINARY EXERCISE
### Mister Rogers' Neighborhood

Who are the special people and where are the special places in your neighborhood? Get to know a whole lot more about the people in your class as you play "musical chairs" and talk about your neighborhood.

1. Who is the "Mister Rogers" in your neighborhood—who likes you just the way you are?
2. Who is the "Mister Goodwrench" in your neighborhood?
3. Who is the most "colorful" person in your neighborhood?
4. Who is the jogger?
5. Who is the "cookie jar" neighbor?
6. Who has the "green thumb"?
7. Who has a fascinating house?
8. Whom would you choose as your "nextdoor neighbor" for life?
9. Where can you go for a quiet walk?
10. Where is the nearest fishing hole?
11. Where is the "fun place" in your neighborhood?
12. Which house would you choose if you could take your choice?
13. What would you like to preserve from your neighborhood for your children to enjoy?
14. What person has done more for your neighborhood than anyone else?
15. What are you going to remember about your neighborhood when you are 75 years old?
16. If you could paint one spot in your neighborhood, what would you paint?

## RELATIONAL BIBLE STUDY
### The Spiritual Blahs

A friend of yours from your high school youth group has come to talk with you. He's married now and living in another town. First read the Scripture and answer the RESEARCH questions below. Then, figure out how you would go about counseling this friend in light of the Scripture passage?

### Streams of Life-Giving Water

*On the last and most important day of the festival* Jesus stood up and said in a loud voice, "Whoever is thirsty should come to me and drink. As the scripture says, 'Whoever believes in me, streams of life-giving water will pour out from his heart.' " Jesus said this about the Spirit, which those who believed in him were going to receive. At that time the Spirit had not yet been given, because Jesus had not been raised to glory.*

*John 7:37-39, GNB*

*The festival was the annual Feast of Tabernacles, which reminded the Jews of their flight from Egypt and 40 years in the wilderness. In the Deeper Bible Study, the tabernacle will be studied in greater detail—to show how each piece of furniture in the tabernacle was symbolic of the work and ministry of Jesus Christ.

**RESEARCH:** Read over the Scripture carefully and complete the questionnaire.

1. **What exactly is Jesus saying in the Scripture passage?**
   a. He (Jesus) is the source of life-giving water
   b. The Holy Spirit will be poured out like water upon all who believe on Christ
   c. The life of the believer will be a channel for the Holy Spirit to flow through to others
   d. The Holy Spirit will "indwell" the believer in such a way that his/her life will "overflow" with his influence

2. **What is the message of hope in this passage for you right now?**
   a. My life does not have to be spiritually dry
   b. God satisfies the thirsty soul
   c. I don't have to make it on my own steam anymore
   d. Life will be different for the person who is centered on Christ
   e. Life without Christ is a spiritual desert
   f. Spiritual deserts are part of any spiritual journey
   g. God meets me in the desert

**CASE HISTORY:** Now, read over the case history of your friend and figure out how you would counsel this friend . . . from the Scripture and from your own experience.

☐ **THE BLAHS:** ". . . Nothin' much is happening. Church is a drag. Everybody has a special little clique. All they talk about is football, the weather, and money. I've lost interest in going. . . ."

☐ **DRYNESS:** "We've replaced the old clunker with a new car. It's a beauty. Our condo is new and modern. All the gadgets are great, but I miss all our old friends that we had at school. When we were in college, we had a Bible study group to go to. Now, we have nothing. . . ."

☐ **HEAVINESS:** ". . . I don't know where God is in all of this. I'm getting dumped on at work. My wife is on my back. Sometimes I wonder if God even cares. I don't know where to turn, or what to do. I want to get out from under all this pressure. . . ."

☐ **LONELINESS:** ". . . I wish I had someone to talk to. My neighbors are as busy as I am and the people at church would not understand. In fact, if my church knew what I was thinking, they would throw me out. . . ."

---

1. **Is there any hope for your friend?**
   a. By all means
   b. I don't know
   c. There must be, but I don't know what
   d. If he wants it

2. **Which struggle of your friend do you identify with right now?**
   a. The blahs
   b. Dryness
   c. Heaviness
   d. Loneliness

3. **In your own spiritual life, how would you counsel yourself?**
   a. Quit dwelling on my problems and start dwelling on Christ
   b. Fill my mind with God so that the Spirit can redirect my steps
   c. Try to discover God's priorities for my life and live by them
   d. Learn the secret of living in harmony with the Spirit
   e. Let God cleanse my heart and move on
   f. Stop worrying about it and let God do his thing

4. **How much of your life is presently under the control of the Spirit?** Put a dot on the line below—somewhere in between 0% and 100%—to indicate how much of your life is under the control of the Spirit.

   0% ________________________________100%

5. **How did you arrive at the decision on the question above?** Check the top three factors by which you measure the "control factor" of the Holy Spirit in your life.
   ____Concern for others
   ____Deep, inner peace and serenity
   ____Victory over sin/selfish desire
   ____Harmony with myself: spirit, mind, and body
   ____Yearning after spiritual things
   ____Joy and celebration
   ____Fruit of the Spirit
   ____Desire for spiritual fellowship
   ____Personal integrity/honesty with self and others
   ____Consistency of spiritual communion

# DEEPER BIBLE STUDY
## About Me . . . and the Christ of the Tabernacle

Let the poem set the stage for the Bible study. Think about Christmas past. Then, dialogue with
God through the Scripture on the meaning of the tabernacle for your life today.

### Christmas Gifts

God, it's been years since we celebrated
    Christmas together and
    I still haven't gotten around
    to unpacking
    the gift you gave me.

It's summer now—
    long dry spells and
    no refreshing rain.

Maybe tomorrow
    I'll get around to unwrapping your gift.

Tell me, God, is there anything important
    in that box
    just for me?

When I think of the Christmas gifts I've never used, I . . .

God, this Christmas I think the present I need most from you is. . . .

## REFLECTION

1. God, when it comes to understanding the "deeper things" of the Spirit, I feel like I'm still
in kindergarten. Is there some way for me to see the Spirit with new eyes? Is there a way to
make the transition from what I do know about you to what I don't know? Is there anyone
who can help me?

*Jesus, then, is the High Priest that meets our needs. . . .*
*The whole point of what we are saying is that we have such a High Priest [Jesus
Christ], who sits at the right of the throne of the Divine Majesty [God Almighty] in heaven. He
serves as high priest in the Most Holy Place, that is, in the real tent which was put up by the
Lord, not by man.*     Hebrews 7:26 and 8:1-2, GNB

To really appreciate the deeper things of the Spirit, I need to understand that Jesus
Christ is. . . .

2. God, you know me. I am not a theologian and I don't know very much about the Bible,
especially when it comes to the Old Testament priesthood and how the tabernacle had
special significance. What was his plan and purpose for all this?

*They serve a copy and shadow of the heavenly sanctuary; for when Moses was about to
erect the tent, he was instructed by God, saying, "See that you make everything according
to the pattern which was shown you on the mountain."*     Hebrews 8:5, RSV

As I understand it, the purpose of the priests and the Old Testament tent was to. . . .

3. I am sorry, God, but I am a little dense when it comes to the things about the Old
Testament priesthood and the connection this has with Jesus Christ. Could you run
through this one more time?

*Now even the first covenant [Old Testament] had regulations for worship and an earthly sanctuary [tabernacle]. For a tent was prepared, the outer one, in which were the LAMPSTAND and the TABLE and the BREAD OF THE PRESENCE; it is called the HOLY PLACE. Behind the second curtain stood a tent called the HOLY OF HOLIES, having the GOLDEN ALTAR OF INCENSE and the ARK OF THE COVENANT covered on all sides with gold, which contained a GOLDEN URN holding the MANNA, and AARON'S ROD that budded, and the TABLES OF THE COVENANT; above it were the CHERUBIM of glory overshadowing the MERCY SEAT.*

*Hebrews 9:1-5, RSV (caps added)*

**The knowledge I have about the tabernacle and the symbolism of Christ in the tabernacle furniture could be put in a. . . .**

## SELF-EXAMINATION

Take the various articles in the tabernacle mentioned in the previous Scripture and jot down a symbol beside each article to indicate your immediate response.

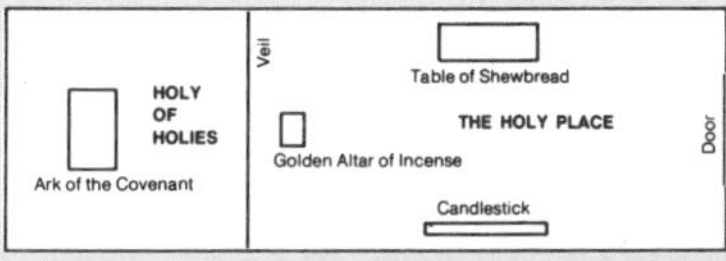


**S** = **Sorry. This does nothing for me.**

**Q** = **Question. I don't understand.**

**I** = **Insight. I never have thought of Christ in this way.**

**W** = **Wow! This is wonderful to think about.**

_______**LAMPSTAND (golden candlestick): The only source of light in the dark tent, symbolizing Christ as the light of the world. The incarnation (coming into the world) of Christ was God's answer to the darkness of mankind.**

_______**TABLE and BREAD OF THE PRESENCE (table of shewbread): Bread made of wheat which was ground into meal and burned in the fire, symbolizing the broken body of Christ who is our source of life, nourishment, and fellowship with God.**

_______**HOLY PLACE: The outer tent where the priests carried out the ritual of daily cleansing, symbolizing the continuing ministry of Christ on our behalf in cleansing us of sins and preparing us for fellowship at God's table.**

_______**HOLY OF HOLIES: The inner tent, separated by a curtain, where the high priest went once a year to make atonement (sacrifice) for sin. When Jesus spoke the words on the cross, "It is finished," the curtain split apart, removing forever the barrier between God and man.**

_______**GOLDEN ALTAR OF INCENSE: The smoke rising from this altar in front of the holy of holies symbolized perpetual praise to God, and the continuous intercession that Jesus Christ offers on our behalf with God in heaven right now.**

_______**ARK OF THE COVENANT: The throne of God inside the holy of holies, made of wood and gold, symbolizing the humanity and divinity of Christ. Inside this chest were the Ten Commandments (God's law), manna, and Aaron's rod that budded like a rose.**

_______**MANNA: A special meal that God provided for the children of Israel on their 40-year journey through the wilderness, symbolizing Christ as the source of our nourishment.**

_______**AARON'S ROD: When the people asked for a sign that Aaron was to be their priest, God made Aaron's stick bud like a rose, symbolizing the resurrection of Jesus Christ as the sign of the new priesthood.**

_______**CHERUBIM: Two angelic figures on top of the ark of the covenant, symbolizing the majesty and holiness of God.**

_______**MERCY SEAT: The lid of the ark of the covenant, where the blood of the atonement (animal sacrifice) was spread as a "covering" for sin, making possible a "meeting place" between God and man. When Christ, the "Lamb of God," died on the cross as a substitute for all sin, he became the eternal "meeting place" for God and man.**

## APPLICATION

Feast for a moment on the conclusion to this whole "perfect work" of Jesus Christ on our behalf. When you are through reading the Scripture, see if you can write a prayer of thanksgiving to God in the open space below. Simply begin with the words "Dear God . . ." and use some of the thoughts from the Scripture in this study.

*Therefore, brethren, since we have confidence to enter the sanctuary by the blood of Jesus, by the new and living way which he opened for us through the curtain, that is, through his flesh, and since we have a great priest over the house of God, let us draw near with a true heart in full assurance of faith, with our hearts sprinkled clean from an evil conscience and our bodies washed with pure water.*

*Hebrews 10:19-22, RSV*

# Comforting

*(Instructions in Leader's Guide)*

## PRELIMINARY EXERCISE

### TV Auction

You've just turned on the TV and discovered the auction of a lifetime. You have $1,000 to bid on all of the items below. Decide on 5 items that you would like to have from this list and divide the $1,000 between these 5 items. Jot down the amount you would bid in the left column under BUDGET for the 5 items. Remember, the total for all 5 items cannot exceed $1,000.

**BUDGET**

______________ **VACATION: All-expenses-paid vacation for two (including air travel) to Disneyland.**

______________ **SUBSCRIPTION: A year's membership in the dating computer-bank, guaranteeing the "perfect" date every weekend.**

______________ **HEALTH CLUB: Lifetime membership to European health spa, guaranteed to build up your sagging muscles.**

______________ **SKIING EXTRAVAGANZA: One month each year of skiing in Vail, Colorado, and the use of your own condo.**

______________ **HASSLE FREE YEAR: A solid year of no hassles at home with your parents/kids/brothers or sisters.**

______________ **CLASSIC CAR: Vintage Masserati automobile to add a touch of class to your driving style.**

______________ **SEASON TICKETS: Your favorite pro team—box seats—plus club card to the players' lounge.**

______________ **TIME OFF: Six months off to do the special things that you've never had time to do.**

______________ **WORLD PEACE: A seat on the U.N. Security Council to work for world peace.**

______________ **SCHOLARSHIP: A full scholarship to return to college and prepare for your dream career.**

______________ **RETIREMENT: A paid-up retirement plan to solve all of your future financial worries.**

______________ **HAPPINESS: One year of happiness when everything seems to go your way.**

## RELATIONAL BIBLE STUDY

### Coping with Stress

Before you get into the Bible study, take a moment and rank how you would cope with the following stress situations from 1 to 10—1 being NO ANXIETY and 10 being HIGH ANXIETY. Beside each situation, jot down a number for your stress factor.

______**DEATH: Your closest friend suddenly dies**

______**SECURITY: One day your boss tells you he's leaving**

______**HOPE SHATTERED: The dreams for the future are dashed**

______**LODGING: You don't have a place to sleep after tonight**

______**REPUTATION: You risked everything and the cause you believed in turns sour**

______**FRIENDS: The old gang breaks up, including most of your friends**

______**SUICIDE: One of the gang hangs himself**

______**BETRAYAL: You feel let down by the one person in the world you trusted**

______**SHAME: The people in town laugh at you and think you've wasted your life**

*"Do not be worried and upset," Jesus told them. "Believe in God and believe also in me. There are many rooms in my Father's house, and I am going to prepare a place for you. I would not tell you this if it were not so. And after I go and prepare a place for you, I will come back and take you to myself, so that you will be where I am. You know the way that leads to the place where I am going."*

*Thomas said to him, "Lord, we do not know where you are going; so how can we know the way to get there?"*

*Jesus answered him, "I am the way, the truth, and the life; no one goes to the Father except by me...."*

**The Promise of the Holy Spirit**

*If you love me, you will obey my commandments. I will ask the Father, and he will give you another Helper, who will stay with you forever. He is the Spirit, who reveals the truth about God. The world cannot receive him, because it cannot see him or know him. But you know him, because he remains with you and is in you....*

*"I have told you this while I am still with you. The Helper, the Holy Spirit, whom the Father will send in my name, will teach you everything and make you remember all that I have told you.*

*"Peace is what I leave with you; it is my own peace that I give you. I do not give it as the world does. Do not be worried and upset; do not be afraid."*

*John 14:1-6, 15-17, 25-27, GNB*

**RESEARCH:** The Scripture is taken from the Last Supper Discourse, on the night before Jesus was crucified . . . and the crises described above actually took place in the lives of the disciples. Read the Scripture carefully and complete the questionnaire.

1. **If you had to face the same crises that the disciples faced, would your faith in God hold up?**
   a. **Yes, my faith has weathered storms like this before**
   b. **No, I don't think my faith would cut it**
   c. **I don't know what I would do**

2. **Which occasion would be most appropriate for this Scripture text?**
   a. **Funeral service: Christ has prepared a new home for us**
   b. **Easter service: Christ arose from death and is coming again**
   c. **Pentecost Sunday: Christ ascended into heaven and sent the Holy Spirit**
   d. **Revival meeting: Christ is the only way to God**

3. **What is especially comforting to you in the Scripture?**
   a. **GOD'S FAITHFULNESS: God will do for me what he has promised**
   b. **COMFORT: God will not leave me in my desolation**
   c. **PEACE: God offers me an inner peace that the world cannot know**
   d. **ASSURANCE: God is still God—no matter what comes**
   e. **HOPE: God has tomorrow for those who put their trust in him.**

**MY OWN STRESS QUOTIENT:** Go back and read the first and last paragraph in the Scripture and see how you come out.

1. **Put a dot on the line—somewhere in between PANIC BUTTON and COMPLETE PEACE—to indicate where you are right now in these areas of your life.**
**CONCERN ABOUT THE FUTURE OF THE COUNTRY: inflation/jobs/housing/schools**
**Panic Button** _________________________________________________ **Complete Peace**
**CONCERN ABOUT THE FUTURE OF MY FAMILY: my parents/kids/jobs/money/retirement**
**Panic Button** _________________________________________________ **Complete Peace**
**CONCERN ABOUT MY OWN FUTURE: job/money/security/advancement/direction**
**Panic Button** _________________________________________________ **Complete Peace**

2. **Let God personalize the last paragraph in the Scripture just for you right now. What would he say? Check the statement that comes the closest to God's message to you.**
   _____ **"Trust me for the future."**
   _____ **"Move over and let me do the driving."**
   _____ **"Learn to wait on me."**
   _____ **"Let me know when you need help."**
   _____ **"Are you through trying to do what I can do for you?"**

# DEEPER BIBLE STUDY
## About Me ... and the Attributes of God

Get in touch with the stress in your life as you read the poem. Dialogue with God about some of your feelings through the Scripture and jot down your responses.

### Abandoned

God, the phone has gone
    dead!

Someone has cut the line
    just when I need you!

I can't go on living this way
    getting "cut off"—
    left hanging in the middle of our conversation.

Can't you do something about this service?

I get panicky when I'm stranded
    with a dead phone in my hand.

Please!

The last time I remember the phone going dead was when. . . .

Spiritually, when the phone goes dead, I. . . .

## REFLECTION

1.  God, if you are really present with me at all times, why do I get crushed by circumstances? Why do you stand by and let these things happen to me?

*The Lord said to me, "Go down to the potter's house, where I will give you my message." So I went there and saw the potter working at his wheel. Whenever a piece of pottery turned out imperfect, he would take the clay and make it into something else.*

*Jeremiah 18:1-4, GNB*

The thought of God working through the circumstances in my life right now really. . . .

2.  God, what are you trying to tell me? I am not a piece of clay. I am not something to be played with.

*But we have this treasure [Christ's Spirit] in earthen vessels, to show that the transcendent power belongs to God and not to us. We are afflicted in every way, but not crushed; perplexed, but not driven to despair; persecuted, but not forsaken; struck down, but not destroyed; always carrying in the body the death of Jesus, so that the life of Jesus may also be manifested in our bodies.*

*2 Corinthians 4:7-10, RSV*

The next time I feel like throwing in the towel, I need to realize that. . . .

## SELF-EXAMINATION

Stress is the result of feeling like all the options are slammed shut. Below are the 14 characteristics of God— called The Attributes of God. Think about each characteristic and circle YES, NO, or MAYBE on the difference this makes in the way you look at yourself.

| | | |
|---|---|---|
| **ALL-KNOWING: God knows everything. There is nothing that can happen in the world without his knowing it.** | Y N M | If God knows everything, God must know what is happening to me right now. |
| **ALL-POWERFUL: God can do anything. There is nothing God cannot do. God is limited only by the limits he sets on himself.** | Y N M | If God is all-powerful, there is no power over my life that he cannot overcome. |
| **CARING: God cares. There is no pain, suffering, or death beyond the reach of God. God is present in pain.** | Y N M | Pain is not for its own sake. God makes it good. |
| **CHANGELESS: God is the one underlying constant in the universe. His being, his character, his Word does not change.** | Y N M | If God is changeless, I can count on the fact he will do what he says he will do. |
| **ETERNAL: God is from everlasting to everlasting. Eternity and God are one and the same.** | Y N M | If God is eternal, then tomorrow can really be a "new" day for me. |
| **FAITHFUL: God is true to himself. God is true to his Word. God is true to his promises.** | Y N M | If God is true to himself, then I can bet my life on this fact. |
| **GLORIOUS: God is all beauty and splendor. His creation is a reflection of his glory.** | Y N M | If I was made in the image of God, I must be beautiful. |
| **GOOD: God is absolute integrity and morality. There is no way God can act except out of goodness.** | Y N M | If God is good, I can trust him to do what is best for me. |
| **HOLY: God is absolute purity. There is no shadow or darkness or evil in his intentions.** | Y N M | If God is holy, he will never do me in. |
| **JUST: God is God, he must be true to his own laws and punish any deviation from his law.** | Y N M | If God is just, I am accepted in Christ's atonement for my sin— forever. |
| **LOVING: God is absolute love, as seen in the gift of his Son, Jesus Christ, to provide for my salvation.** | Y N M | Regardless of how I feel about myself, I am loved. |
| **MAJESTIC: God is all-encompassing. Awe-inspiring. Beyond definition. The beginning, middle, and end of all creation.** | Y N M | If God and all his creation is awe-inspiring, then I must be too. |
| **MERCIFUL: God is limitless in compassion. His kindness is from everlasting to everlasting.** | Y N M | If God is merciful, I can admit my mistakes and not get obliterated. |
| **SOVEREIGN: God is the only God there is. Whatever he wills to do he can do. He is the ruler and sustainer of the universe.** | Y N M | If God is sovereign, I don't have to worry about anything anymore. |

## APPLICATION

Now, back to your own life for a moment. Read slowly the Scripture, pausing after each sentence to repeat the refrain:

**"But God, I want to tell you about my own problems."**

Remember, read a sentence and then repeat the refrain. See what happens. The words of Scripture are the last words of King David before his death.

*There in front of the whole assembly King David praised the Lord. He said, "Lord God of our ancestor Jacob, may you be praised forever and ever! You are great and powerful, glorious, splendid, and majestic. Everything in heaven and earth is yours, and you are king, supreme ruler over all. All riches and wealth come from you; you rule everything by your strength and power; and you are able to make anyone great and strong. Now, our God, we give you thanks, and we praise your glorious name."*    *1 Chronicles 29:10-13, GNB*

# Abiding

*(Instructions in Leader's Guide)*

## PRELIMINARY EXERCISE
### Botanical Garden

Below is a list of flowers, shrubs, and trees that you might find in a botanical garden. Think of the people in your group as you read over the list and pick one for each person in your group. Jot down, their names next to the item that you feel is close to the individual's personality.

__________ **BURSTING SUNFLOWER: exuberant, effervescent, giver of sunshine and nourishing seeds with all sorts of energy.**

__________ **SHY, DELICATE VIOLET: sensitive, refreshingly natural—often found along the beaten path—a traveler's delight.**

__________ **WILD ROSE: untamed, unpretentious, rambling, flourishing along country lanes and unexpected places.**

__________ **STURDY, DESERT CACTUS: with unbelievable tenacity to overcome adverse elements—giving natural beauty to the desert.**

__________ **GLORIOUS EASTER LILY: dramatic, symbolic of resurrection and new life, of hope and courage.**

__________ **WHITE DAISY: bright, happy, with a quiet fragrance—innocent and irresistible. A harbinger of love.**

__________ **GIANT CORSAGE CHRYSANTHEMUM: bold, vivid, bursting with inner beauty—extravagant and outrageous.**

__________ **TALL MAJESTIC OAK: stalwart, deep-rooted, rough-textured on the outside, strong on the inside. Endures raging storms.**

__________ **ROYAL PALM TREE: complete with succulent coconuts—found along shorelines of exotic islands.**

__________ **CHRISTMAS TREE: radiant, life-sharing, joy-giving—brightly decorated, childlike and exciting.**

__________ **YEAR-AROUND EVERGREEN: consistent, never-changing—able to thrive in rocky soil and harsh, cold environments.**

__________ **HARDY BUTTERCUP: modest, unassuming, old-fashioned, enduring, and very special.**

__________ **COLORADO ASPEN: shimmering, vivacious, colorful, found in the high country—brilliant and gloriously alive.**

__________ **GRAPEVINE: source of joy, gaiety, vitality, and life. Lives only to give itself away.**

---

**JESUS SAID:**

*"I am the real vine, and my Father is the gardener. He breaks off every branch in me that does not bear fruit, and he prunes every branch that does bear fruit, so that it will be clean and bear more fruit. You have been made clean already by the teaching I have given you. Remain united to me, and I will remain united to you. A branch cannot bear fruit by itself; it can do so only if it remains in the vine. In the same way you cannot bear fruit unless you remain in me.*

*"I am the vine, and you are the branches. Whoever remains in me, and I in him, will bear much fruit; for you can do nothing without me."*     *John 15:1-5, GNB*

The grapevine was a common sight in biblical times. Jesus used the grapevine and the wine produced from the grape to symbolize a life full of joy.

# RELATIONAL BIBLE STUDY

## The Secret of Fruitfulness

One of the most familiar Scripture passages in the Bible is the vine and branch allegory. Here's a chance to find out what God might be saying to you about your own spiritual condition.

**RESEARCH:** Read the Scripture carefully for the basic significance and teaching about a "Spirit-filled" life.

**1. How much do you know about gardening, particularly wine-producing grapevines?**
    **a. A lot        b. A little        c. I am embarrassed to say**

**2. For those who are embarrassed to say, make a drawing of a grapevine. Then, based on the Scripture and your drawing, answer the statements below TRUE, FALSE or DON'T KNOW.**

T F ?   **The life of the grape is in the branch.**
T F ?   **A good gardener is a tough pruner.**
T F ?   **Pruning a vine will not hurt it.**
T F ?   **It's the job of the branch to stay tied to the vine.**
T F ?   **If you do not bear spiritual fruit, you are going to be burned alive.**
T F ?   **You can't judge a grapevine by its looks.**
T F ?   **Abiding in the vine takes a lot of work on the part of the branch.**
T F ?   **A busy life is often barren of fruit.**
T F ?   **A mature grapevine takes years of growing.**
T F ?   **If a branch gets too much fruit on it, it will be overloaded.**

**MY OWN STORY:** Think back over your own spiritual life and try to identify four times in your own experience.

**PLANTING: First time my spiritual roots were put in the ground or took root.**

**FRUIT-BEARING: Best fruit-bearing season of your life.**

**PRUNING: First time you recall being pruned by God.**

**BAD YEAR: The worst season for fruit/joy in your life.**

**PRUNING:** Focus on the pruning experience above and try to identify these lessons: What exactly necessitated the "pruning"?
    **a. the barrenness of a busy life**
    **b. made some bad decisions**
    **c. pride in my own accomplishments**
    **d. laziness**
    **e. _______________________**

**FRUIT-BEARING:** Focus on the best year in your life and try to identify the reason. What exactly caused the fruit?
    **a. a deep spiritual community**
    **b. deeper spiritual experience**
    **c. consistent devotional life**
    **d. hard work**
    **e. _______________________**

**THIS SEASON'S CROP:** Focus on the last six months and put a dot on the line—somewhere in between CROP FAILURE and BUMPER CROP—to indicate what this season has been like for deep spiritual fruit.

**Crop Failure** _________________________________________ **Bumper Crop**

# DEEPER BIBLE STUDY

### About Me ... and the Fruit of the Spirit

Get in touch with your own "Poor Me" feelings as you read over the Bible study. Then, move into the Scripture and dialogue with God about anything on your spiritual agenda ... or his.

**Poor Me**

| | |
|---|---|
| Lord, I am | **SO TIRED** |
| giving | **SO MUCH** |
| for | **SO LONG** |
| to | **SO MANY** |
| with | **SO LITTLE** |
| that I am | **WORN OUT** |
| doing the | **IMPOSSIBLE** |
| for the | **UNGRATEFUL** |
| who expect | **EVERYTHING** |
| for | **NOTHING** |

**I generally get these feelings when....**

**The best medicine for me when I get this way is to....**

## REFLECTION

**1. God, let's face it. I'm worn out. I've given everything I've got. I keep going—from morning to night—trying to do what you want of me, but I don't have anything anymore. What do I do now?**

*Do not get drunk with wine, which will only ruin you; instead, be filled with the Spirit.*
*Ephesians 5:18, GNB*

**I wasn't planning on getting drunk anyway, but the analogy here is intriguing. The point I see in this comparison to wine and drunkenness is....**

**2. God, what does it mean to be "filled with the Spirit" anyway? Am I some kind of vessel that you can pour the Spirit into? I really want to turn over my life to the Spirit, but I don't know how.**

*Those who live as the Spirit tells them to, have their minds controlled by what the Spirit wants.... To be controlled by the Spirit results in life and peace.*
*Romans 8:5-6, GNB*

**As I understand it, to be filled by the Spirit means....**

**3. God, I don't want to appear dense about the Holy Spirit, but I am still confused. What exactly do I have to do to be "filled with the Spirit," and second, if I am "filled with the Spirit," how is this going to make a difference in my life?**

*Those who are led by God's Spirit are God's sons. For the Spirit that God has given you does not make you slaves and cause you to be afraid; instead, the Spirit makes you God's children, and by the Spirit's power we cry out to God, "Father! my Father!" God's Spirit joins himself to our spirits to declare that we are God's children. Since we are his children, we will possess the blessings he keeps for his people, and we will also possess with Christ what God has kept for him; for if we share Christ's suffering, we will also share his glory.*
*Romans 8:14-17, GNB*

In answer to my two questions:
**What do I have to do to be "filled with the Spirit"? The answer is. . . .**

**How does this make a difference in my life? The answer is. . . .**

## SELF-EXAMINATION

To help you get a handle on what kind of a difference the Holy Spirit can make in your life, take each "fruit of the Spirit" described in Galatians 5:22-23 and check yourself. On a scale of 1 to 10—1 being very low and 10 being very high—circle the number that indicates how you see yourself right now in relationship to the Holy Spirit's ideal for you.

**LOVE: Unconditional acceptance of others, no strings attached, no anticipated "payoff," no attempt to control or manipulate others—especially those you love the most.**

1 2 3 4 5 6 7 8 9 10

**JOY: Spontaneous, effervescent cheerfulness, flowing from deep spiritual reservoirs—especially in times of strain, stress, and heartache.**

1 2 3 4 5 6 7 8 9 10

**PEACE: Inner harmony, soundness, well-being, at-one-ment with God that makes possible a spirit of reconciliation in the midst of conflict—especially among those in your own family.**

1 2 3 4 5 6 7 8 9 10

**PATIENCE: Strength of will in the midst of trying circumstances and exasperating people—not easily threatened when things don't go your way.**

1 2 3 4 5 6 7 8 9 10

**KINDNESS: Sensitivity and compassion for those who are hurting, sympathy and empathy for those who are having a bad day—especially those in your own family and spiritual community.**

1 2 3 4 5 6 7 8 9 10

**GOODNESS: Disposition to do what is right, fair, honorable, and honest; integrity; 14-carat character; champion of truth, justice, and principles—even if you have to stand alone or against your friends.**

1 2 3 4 5 6 7 8 9 10

**FAITHFULNESS: unwavering, constant, genuine fidelity to what you value, believe and cherish—being true to yourself at the cost of friends, job, and reputation.**

1 2 3 4 5 6 7 8 9 10

**HUMILITY: Genuine meekness (not weakness), gentleness, tenderness. Healthy self-esteem that does not have to put on airs or try to impress anyone— ANYONE—especially those you are thinking of right now.**

1 2 3 4 5 6 7 8 9 10

**SELF-CONTROL: Aware of your strengths and weaknesses; in control of your doubts or illusions of grandeur; open to the Spirit but suspicious of your motives; master of your physical/sexual desires.**

1 2 3 4 5 6 7 8 9 10

## APPLICATION

If you have been honest, you have probably felt a sense of "what's the use trying" in the Self-Examination. This is healthy. It shows you are sensitive . . . and open to the new thing that God is doing in you by speaking to your spiritual yearning.

To close out this session, take a few minutes and feast on the Scripture below and turn the words of Scripture into your own prayer.

*For this reason I bow my knees before the Father, from whom every family in heaven and on earth is named, that according to the riches of his glory he may grant you to be strengthened with might through his Spirit in the inner man, and that Christ may dwell in your hearts through faith; that you, being rooted and grounded in love, may have power to comprehend with all the saints what is the breadth and length and height and depth, and to know the love of Christ which surpasses knowledge, that you may be filled with all the fulness of God.*

*Ephesians 3:14-19 RSV*

# Guiding

*(Instructions in Leader's Guide)*

## PRELIMINARY EXERCISE
### Once-in-a-Lifetime Party

Guess what? You're going to have a party—for yourself. A once-in-a-lifetime party for the reunion of old friends and special people who have made your life full. If you had an unlimited budget, what would you plan?

Get together with one other person and plan your party, using the interview questions below.

1.  **Invitation list: who would be invited?**
    - ☐ **Close friend in your childhood**
    - ☐ **Favorite teacher/coach who had a great impact on you**
    - ☐ **Person who influenced your early spiritual life**
    - ☐ **Person who stood by you in time of crisis/heartache**
    - ☐ **Significant person in your life now**
2.  **Place: where would you hold the party?**
3.  **Entertainment: what would you have for music/entertainment?**
4.  **Decorations: how would you decorate the place?**
5.  **Toasts: what would you give in the way of gifts or toasts to each guest?**

## RELATIONAL BIBLE STUDY
### The Ministry of the Holy Spirit

There is a lot of confusion about the purpose and ministry of the Holy Spirit today. This study will give you a chance to focus on a Scripture that describes this ministry in detail.

**RESEARCH:** Read over the Scripture for clues to the ministry of the Holy Spirit.

**JESUS SAID:**

*"The Helper will come—the Spirit, who reveals the truth about God and who comes from the Father. I will send him to you from the Father, and he will speak about me. And you, too, will speak about me, because you have been with me from the very beginning...."*

**The Work of the Holy Spirit**

*"But I am telling you the truth: it is better for you that I go away, because if I do not go, the Helper will not come to you. But if I do go away, then I will send him to you. And when he comes, he will prove to the people of the world that they are wrong about sin and about what is right and about God's judgment. They are wrong about sin, because they do not believe in me; they are wrong about what is right, because I am going to the Father and you will not see me any more; and they are wrong about judgment, because the ruler of this world has already been judged."*

*John 15:26-27; 16:7-11, GNB*

1. Based on the evidence in the Scripture, which image comes closest to the way you see the ministry of the Holy Spirit?: (pick two)

    a. **Personal Tutor:** to teach you about the things of God

    b. **Radar Signal:** to keep you on target

    c. **Front-Row Prompter:** to coach you when you forget who you are on stage

    d. **Guardian:** to take the place of Jesus Christ as spiritual caretaker after Jesus ascends to heaven

    e. **Pediatrician:** to keep a constant watch on your spiritual development

    f. **The Matchmaker (Fiddler on the Roof):** to bring you and God together in spiritual marriage

2. In particular, the ministry of the Holy Spirit is described in three ways. What does each mean? Circle the statements that come the closest to your understanding: *And when he comes, he will prove to the people of the world that (1) they are wrong about sin, (2) what is right, and (3) about God's judgment. . . .*

*"They are wrong about sin"* means:

☐ The Holy Spirit will convict you of the unforgivable sin of self-righteousness—thinking you've done nothing wrong to deserve judgment.

☐ The Holy Spirit will make you sensitive to the sin in your life that is keeping you from fellowship with God.

☐ The Holy Spirit will help you to see sin as Jesus did, and not as the hypocritical Pharisees.

☐ The Holy Spirit will help you to believe in all that Jesus did and who he is.

*"About what is right"* means:

☐ The Holy Spirit will lead you to live a life that pleases God after Jesus goes to be with the Father.

☐ The Holy Spirit will help you to understand that right standing with God comes through Jesus Christ.

☐ The Holy Spirit will let you know whenever you have done something that is unloving, unjust, or unfaithful to God.

☐ The Holy Spirit will walk with you as Jesus did with the disciples—teaching you daily about life and real living.

*"And about God's judgment"* means:

☐ The Holy Spirit will teach you how God dealt with your sin once and for all through the death of Christ.

☐ The Holy Spirit will show you how the rule of evil was broken and that sin does not have power over you.

☐ The Holy Spirit will assure you that the guilt problem is gone and there is no future judgment.

☐ The Holy Spirit will convict you of the fact that if you are not actively for God, you are against God.

**MY OWN EXPERIENCE:** If you had to illustrate the work and ministry of the Holy Spirit from your own experience, what would you say?

1. How does the Holy Spirit go about leading you? Rank the top three influences in making daily decisions.

    _____getting spiritual counsel from friends

    _____reading the Scripture

    _____being alone with God

    _____thinking through decisions logically

    _____belonging to a support group

    _____waiting on God to speak direct

    _____the witness of "inner peace" that what I am doing is right

    _____stepping out "in faith" and letting God open or close doors

    _____listening for the "cry" of human needs

    _____living as you think Christ would live in your situation

2. Which of these biblical stories comes the closest to your own experience of the Holy Spirit?

    a. The "faithful servant" that Abraham sent to find a "bride" for his son Isaac (Gen. 24). ". . . To seek, find, choose, prepare, and present the bride."

    b. The "still small voice" that comforted Elijah after his faith crumbled at the threat of Jezebel on his life (1 Kings 19).

    c. The "voice" that spoke to Saul (Paul) on the road to Damascus (Acts 9).

    d. The "angel" that whispered in the night to Paul (before the shipwreck) that he would survive the storm (Acts 27).

3. **How active is the Holy Spirit right now in directing your life?**
(Put a dot on the line to indicate the relationship.)

**He's on vacation** _________________________________ **He's on the phone right now**

# DEEPER BIBLE STUDY
## About Me ... and Spiritual Leading
Get in touch with where you are in the poem and move on to dialogue with God in the Scripture about the next steps in your spiritual life.

### Footprints

God, what happened?

Suddenly, I'm going nowhere,
    wandering
    aimlessly,
    trying to pick up
    signs
    of your footprints—
    and nothing's here, there—anywhere!

Send up a flare.
Give a holler.
Show me a sign.
Do something—anything.
God, I'm lost!

The first time I can remember getting lost was....

If I had a compass to take a reading on my spiritual life right now, it would be....

## REFLECTION

1. God, when I look at my spiritual life, I get depressed. I seem to be going nowhere—fast. The current is so swift, and the forces so strong. Are you sure there is any hope for me?

*The Lord says "... I alone know the plans I have for you, plans to bring you prosperity and not disaster, plans to bring about the future you hope for.... You will seek me, and you will find me because you will seek me with all your heart."*     Jeremiah 29:10-13, GNB

The words in these verses that really speak to me are....

2. God, I don't see any light at the end of the tunnel. Some days I can't see the sun at all. Some nights all I feel is cold hard pain. I'm in bondage to my worst enemy—myself.

*You will leave Babylon* with joy;*
    *you will be led out of the city in peace.*
*The mountains and hills will burst into singing,*
    *and the trees will shout for joy.*
*Cypress trees will grow where now there are briers;*
    *myrtle trees will come up in place of thorns.*
*This will be a sign that will last forever,*
    *a reminder of what I, the Lord, have done.*     Isaiah 55:12-13, GNB

When I think of my own spiritual life in these terms, I....

God's promises mean most to me when....

*Babylon, the capital of the Babylonian Empire, symbolizes captivity because the children of Israel in the Old Testament were taken as prisoners to Babylon for 70 years.

## SELF-EXAMINATION

Bob Munger, a tremendous man of God, in his little booklet, "My Heart—Christ's Home," describes the various areas of our life as the rooms of a house. These areas are controlled by the Spirit/God . . . or the world/flesh. In your imaginaton, walk through the rooms of your life with Christ as your guide and ask yourself at each room, "Is this room in my life filled with God?" For each room, award the "Good Housekeeping Seal of Approval."

    ***** = **barely passing, needs cleaning**
   ****** = **passing, but needs dusting**
  ******* = **good rating, but could be touched up**
 ******** = **excellent, nothing to improve on**

☐ **LIBRARY: This room is your mind— what you allow to go into it and come out of it. It is the "control room" of the entire house.**

☐ **WORKSHOP: This room is where your gifts, talents, skills are put to work for the Lord. Your workshop runs by the power of the Spirit.**

☐ **DINING ROOM: Appetites, desires, those things that your mind and spirit feed on for nourishment as you sit at this table.**

☐ **RUMPUS ROOM: The social area of your life, and the things you do to amuse and entertain yourself and others.**

☐ **DRAWING ROOM: The room where you draw close to God, seek time with him daily—not sporadically or only in times of distress or need.**

☐ **HALL CLOSET: The one secret, hidden place that no one knows about, but is a real stumbling block in your walk in the Spirit.**

## APPLICATION

As a practical step, why not write out the Scripture verse below on a 3 x 5 card and tape it on the refrigerator or bathroom mirror. Every time you see this card this week, read it over slowly and allow the passage to "fill your thoughts."

To start the process, meditate on the verse and try to rephrase the words IN YOUR OWN EVERYDAY SPEECH in the space below.

For instance, for the first phrase, "whatever is true," you might jot down, "whatever I know is truth—the things I believe in, value, and cherish," etc.

Just start writing the verse as it is. After each phrase, write "that is" and try to put the thought into your own words—several different ways. Before long, you will find the thoughts coming so quickly you can hardly write them down fast enough.

*Finally, brethren, whatever is true, whatever is honorable, whatever is just, whatever is pure, whatever is lovely, whatever is gracious, if there is any excellence, if there is anything worthy of praise, think about these things.*
*Philippians 4:8, RSV*

# Empowering

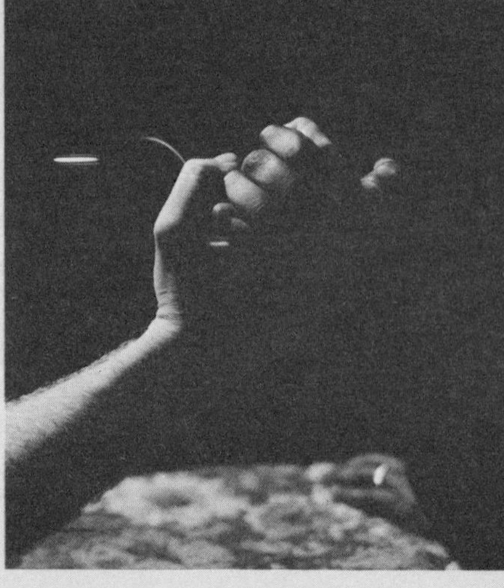

*(Instructions in Leader's Guide)*

## PRELIMINARY EXERCISE
### Aladdin's Lamp
You have found Aladdin's magic lamp. As you rub it, a genie appears and grants you three wishes. Look over the list below and pick the three wishes you would want most.

____**HIGH-PAYING JOB: never have to worry about bills again**

____**ONE ABIDING FRIENDSHIP: a friend who will stick with you forever**

____**STRESS-FREE LIFE: a life free of struggle and strife, tension and pain**

____**TRAVEL: an all-expenses-paid trip around the world**

____**CLOSE FAMILY: a family bond that is lasting, secure, and affirming**

____**GOOD HEALTH: long life full of vitality and well-being**

____**WORLDWIDE RECOGNITION: success and fame in your chosen field**

____**HAPPINESS: a life full of joy and fulfillment**

____**WEALTH: a vast fortune to spend any way you want to**

____**CONTRIBUTION: a chance to make a contribution to mankind**

____**DIRECTION NOW: to know what you want to do with the rest of your life**

____**A SATISFYING FAITH: a fulfilling spiritual life**

## RELATIONAL BIBLE STUDY
### Equipped to Be Sent
A lot of confusion surrounds the work of the Holy Spirit in the life of the Christian today. To clear up any misunderstanding, let's go back and study the three events that led up to Pentecost . . . and see how they work together.

**RESEARCH:** Read the three Scripture passages below carefully and jot down the gist of each part in the boxes below in outline form:

| COMMAND | PROMISE | COMMENCEMENT |
|---|---|---|
|  |  |  |

**Jesus Appears to His Disciples After His Resurrection**
COMMAND: *The eleven disciples went to the hill in Galilee where Jesus had told them to go. When they saw him, they worshiped him, even though some of them doubted. Jesus drew near and said to them, "I have been given all authority in heaven and on earth. Go, then, to all peoples everywhere and make them my disciples: baptize them in the name of the Father, the Son, and the Holy Spirit, and teach them to obey everything I have commanded you. And I will be with you always, to the end of the age."*

*Matthew 28:16-20, GNB*

**Jesus Is Taken Up to Heaven**
PROMISE: *When the apostles met together with Jesus, they asked him, "Lord, will you at this time give the Kingdom back to Israel?"*

*Jesus said to them, "The times and occasions are set by my Father's own authority, and it is not for you to know when they will be. But when the Holy Spirit comes upon you, you will be filled with power, and you will be witnesses for me in Jerusalem, in all of Judea and Samaria, and to the ends of the earth." After saying this, he was taken up to heaven as they watched him, and a cloud hid him from their sight.*

*Acts 1:6-9, GNB*

**The Coming of the Holy Spirit**
COMMENCEMENT: *When the day of Pentecost came, all the believers were gathered together in one place. Suddenly there was a noise from the sky which sounded like a strong wind blowing, and it filled the whole house where they were sitting. Then they saw what looked like tongues of fire which spread out and touched each person there. They were all filled with the Holy Spirit and began to talk in other languages, as the Spirit enabled them to speak....*

*Then Peter stood up with the other eleven apostles and spoke.... "These people are not drunk, as you suppose; it is only nine o'clock in the morning. Instead, this is what the prophet Joel spoke about:*
*'This is what I will do in the last days, God says:*
*I will pour out my Spirit on everyone.*
*Your sons and daughters will proclaim my message;*
*your young men will see visions,*
*and your old men will have dreams....'"*

*Acts 2:1-4, 14-17, GNB*

Now, go back and focus on the last Scripture (Acts 2) and fill in these particular facts. Again, jot down key words.

| What were they doing? | What happened? | How did Peter explain it? |
| --- | --- | --- |
| | | |

**MY OWN STORY:** Compare your notes about the Scripture to your own experience.

1. In comparison to the experience of the disciples at Pentecost, my experience with the Holy Spirit has been:
   a. Rather tame
   b. Different, but just as real
   c. More like Peter's explanation

2. The thing that jumps out to me in these Scripture passages is:
   a. The connection between the Great Commission (command) and the Holy Spirit's coming
   b. The connection between the Holy Spirit and big dreams and visions
   c. The unity of the community before the Spirit came
   d. The waiting period—10 days—getting ready
   e. The sign of the Holy Spirit through "other languages"
   f. _______________________________

3. For me right now, I feel like I am somewhere in between: (put a dot where you are)

Waiting for the Spirit to come to me _____________________________ Living in the faith that the Spirit has already come

# DEEPER BIBLE STUDY

## About Me ... and My Spiritual Gift

Get in touch with your own feelings as you read the poem and dialogue with God about your spiritual gift. Allow the Scripture to speak and jot down your responses.

### Cry Baby

**God, get somebody else—please!**

I can't speak like Peter.
I can't think like Paul.
I can't write like Moses.
I can't work like Martha.
I can't give like Solomon.
I can't lead like David.
I can't pray like Mary.
I can't teach like Matthew.
I can't care like Hosea.
I can't manage like Joseph.
I can't obey like Abraham.
I can't wait like Job.
I can't love like .... you!

**Please, God, get somebody else!**

I get to feeling this way when....

I feel the gift I have to contribute to Christ and his work is....

## REFLECTION

1. God, this whole idea of having a "spiritual gift" is a mystery to me. The only people that talk about this are "charismatics" and all they talk about is "tongues." Frankly, God, I'm not sure I want to get into this problem.

*Now concerning spiritual gifts, brethren, I do not want you to be uninformed....*
*There are varieties of gifts.... To one is given through the Spirit the utterance of wisdom, and to another ... knowledge ... to another faith ... to another gifts of healing ... to another the working of miracles, to another prophecy, to another the ability to distinguish between spirits, to another various kinds of tongues, to another the interpretation of tongues. All these are inspired by one and the same Spirit, who apportions to each one individually as he wills.* 1 Corinthians 12:1, 4-11, RSV

My first reaction when I read this Scripture in all honesty is....

2. What in the samhill are these gifts for anyway?

*It was he [God] who "gave gifts to mankind...." He did this to prepare all God's people for the work of Christian service, in order to build up the body of Christ.* Ephesians 4:11-12, GNB

The whole value and purpose of spiritual gifts is to....

3. Why all the fuss about "spiritual gifts" anyway? I have gotten along for years without knowing what my "gift" is, why do I have to start now? It never seemed to bother anybody else!

*Do not be conformed to this world but be transformed by the renewal of your mind, that you may prove [find out] what is the will of God.... For as in one body we have many members, and all the members do not have the same function, so we, though many, are one body in Christ, and individually members one of another. Having gifts that differ according to the grace given to us, let us use them....* Romans 12:2, 4-6, RSV

> **If knowing what the "will of God" is for my life, and knowing what "my gift" is are interrelated, then I'd better. . . .**

## SELF-EXAMINATION

Below are two lists that need to be considered at the same time. In the left column, the SPIRITUAL GIFTS that are described in Romans 12:6-8. In the right column, the BODY NEEDS for a functioning community.

For the SPIRITUAL GIFTS, check one gift that you feel comes the closest to your basic personality or inner drive.

For the BODY NEEDS, jot down the names of the people in your group next to the job or function that you feel each person is most qualified (by spiritual gift) to fill.

**SPIRITUAL GIFTS** (check the one closest to your basic personality).

☐ **THE PROPHET: Talk-oriented. Forthright, outspoken, and strong-willed. A natural-born leader. Good talker/poor listener. Dogmatic, strong convictions, uncompromising. Sometimes hard to live with; insensitive to other's feelings, hard-nosed, and a little overpowering.**

☐ **THE SERVANT: Practical-needs-oriented. Hard-working, conscientious, and faithful. Natural-born helper—behind the scenes. Gets satisfaction out of seeing things done, regardless of who gets the credit. Often gets overextended and overworked to the neglect of his or her own spiritual life. Can get the "self-pities" and "bitchy."**

☐ **THE TEACHER: Concept-oriented. Systematic, logical, and theoretical. A natural-born word processor. Good at careful, painstaking research, organizing data, and writing books and sermons—sometimes interesting. Can get a little "stuffy," cloistered, unrelated to people and even a little "proud" of accomplishments.**

☐ **THE EXHORTER: Success-oriented. Self-disciplined, single-minded, completely dedicated. A natural-born coach in the Tom Landry style. Good at** setting goals, and helping others achieve their goals. **Can be a little demanding, hard on self . . . and hard on others, particularly when results aren't readily seen. Easily discouraged when his or her expectations are not fulfilled.**

☐ **THE GIVER (PHILANTHROPIST): Cause-oriented. Analyst, strategist, natural-born investment broker. Able to see the "big picture," assess resources, accumulate wealth and use it wisely. Easily upset by the misuse of time, talent, and resources in the church. Desperately needed, but seldom appreciated.**

☐ **THE ADMINISTRATOR: Task-oriented. Organized, authoritative, decisive, and thrives under pressure. Good at delegating responsibility and getting things done through others. Can be a little insensitive, manipulative, and "pushy" when the task demands it.**

☐ **THE SYMPATHIZER: Feeling-oriented. Highly sensitive to others in need, compassionate and affirming. Good at listening, caring, and "being present" when someone is hurting. This kind of person can be easily "hurt," emotionally drained, and/or make people "dependent" on them.**

**BODY NEEDS** (Jot down the people in your group next to the job they could best fill)

_______________ **WORSHIP LEADER: directing our thoughts to God at the beginning and end of the group sessions.**

_______________ **SHEPHERD: being sensitive to anyone who is really hurting and directing us into times of healing.**

_______________ **SPIRITUAL DIRECTOR: holding us accountable for our common spiritual disciplines, such as prayer, meditation, and study.**

_______________ **EVANGELIST: keeping before all of us the need to reach out, touch, share our lives and our faith.**

_______________ **MISSION DIRECTOR: confronting us with the needs of others beyond our community.**

_______________ **CELEBRATION PLANNER: calling us to be a joyous people, remembering birthdays, special times, and good times.**

_______________ **MODERATOR: keeping all of the above in balance, correcting our course when we lose our way.**

## APPLICATION

Let's conclude our study of spiritual gifts the way the Apostle Paul concludes his discussion in 1 Corinthians. Read the passage slowly, and let your mind walk through the Scripture into a time of prayer.

> *But earnestly desire the higher gifts.*
> *And I will show you a still more excellent way.*
> *If I speak in the tongues of men and of angels, but have not love, I am a noisy gong or a clanging cymbal. And if I have prophetic powers, and understand all mysteries and all knowledge, and if I have all faith, so as to remove mountains, but have not love, I am nothing. If I give away all I have, and if I deliver my body to be burned, but have not love, I gain nothing. . . .*
> *So faith, hope, love abide, these three; but the greatest of these is love."*
>
> *1 Corinthians 12:31 and 13:1-3, 13, RSV*

# Come, Holy Spirit

*(Instructions in Leader's Guide)*

## PRELIMINARY EXERCISE
### Pick a Promise

Take your pick. Read over the list of special promises in Scripture below and check the one you want to have especially for the days ahead.

☐ *... I am sure that God, who began this good work in you, will carry it on until it is finished on the Day of Christ Jesus.*　　Philippians 1:6, GNB

☐ *Call to me, and I will answer you; I will tell you wonderful and marvelous things that you know nothing about.*　　Jeremiah 33:3, GNB

☐ *Do not cling to events of the past or dwell on what happened long ago. Watch for the new thing I am going to do. It is happening already—you can see it now! I will make a road through the wilderness and give you streams of water there.*　　Isaiah 43:18-19, GNB

☐ *And God is able to give you more than you need, so that you will always have all you need for yourselves and more than enough for every good cause.*　　2 Corinthians 9:8, GNB

☐ *I have the strength to face all conditions by the power that Christ gives me.*　　Philippians 4:13, GNB

☐ *When anyone is joined to Christ, he is a new being; the old is gone, the new has come.*　　2 Corinthians 5:17, GNB

☐ *We know that in all things God works for good with those who love him, those whom he has called according to his purpose.*　　Romans 8:28, GNB

☐ *Those who trust in the Lord for help will find their strength renewed. They will rise on wings like eagles; they will run and not get weary; they will walk and not grow weak.*　　Isaiah 40:31, GNB

☐ *Ask, and you will receive; seek, and you will find; knock, and the door will be opened to you. For everyone who asks will receive, and anyone who seeks will find, and the door will be opened to him who knocks.*　　Matthew 7:7, GNB

☐ *Every test that you have experienced is the kind that normally comes to people. But God keeps his promise, and he will not allow you to be tested beyond your power to remain firm; at the time you are put to the test, he will give you the strength to endure it, and so provide you with a way out.*　　1 Corinthians 10:13, GNB

☐ *Listen! I stand at the door and knock; if anyone hears my voice and opens the door, I will come into his house and eat with him, and he will eat with me.*　　Revelation 3:20, GNB

□ *Who . . . can separate us from the love of Christ? Can trouble do it, or hardship or persecution or hunger or poverty or danger or death?. . . No, in all these things we have complete victory through him who loved us! For I am certain that nothing can separate us from his love: neither death nor life, neither angels nor other heavenly rulers or powers, neither the present nor the future, neither the world above nor the world below—there is nothing in all creation that will ever be able to separate us from the love of God which is ours through Christ Jesus our Lord.*
*Romans 8:35-38, GNB*

□ *I will always guide you and satisfy you with good things. I will keep you strong and well. You will be like a garden that has plenty of water, like a spring of water that never goes dry.*
*Isaiah 58:11, GNB*

## EVALUATION EXERCISE
### Seasons Of The Soul
Turn back to page 5 and check the "season" of your spiritual life for each category. Use the boxes in the RIGHT COLUMN this time.

If you did not complete this exercise at the beginning of the course, don't worry about it. Do the checkup anyway.

## WRAP-UP EXERCISE
### You've Come a Long Way
1. If I had to describe my experience during this course, it would be: (choose one)
   a. One small step
   b. The raising of the *Titanic*
   c. The hills are alive with the sound of music
   d. Warming trend forecasted
   e. I can't believe I ate the whole thing
   f. I thunk I was alone, but I ain't
   g. Roll over, Beethoven, I'm into the "Rock"
   h. Play it again, Sam
   i. Free at last! Free at last!
   j. Overwhelmed and on the way

2. The thing that stands out in my memory is the:
   a. Deep fellowship
   b. Fun times
   c. Bible study
   d. Prayer
   e. Sharing
   f. Belonging to real people
   g. Mind-blowing insights
   h. Quiet change in me
   i. New freedom to the Spirit

3. I think God is calling me to:
   a. Trust him in a deeper way in my daily life
   b. Get up and get going
   c. Move over and give him the reins
   d. Start with myself
   e. See the world through his eyes
   f. Do something crazy for a change

4. If I am going to take God seriously, it is going to mean:
   a. A complete overhaul of my priorities
   b. All the support I can get from friends
   c. Dealing with the hang-up in my life
   d. Getting into Scripture daily
   e. Forgetting about my fears
   f. Starting all over again

## ABOUT THE AUTHOR

The subject of the Holy Spirit is like an elephant. It is hard to get hold of.

This is probably why I saved this course for last. I needed time to get a hold.

### My Background

You need to know where I'm coming from on this subject. It will help to explain why I have dealt with the subject of the Holy Spirit as I have.

I grew up in an old-fashioned Methodist Church in the South where the Holy Spirit was emphasized, in the style of John Wesley. Revival meetings. Heavy preaching about sin: "Getting right with God . . . praying through to victory . . . the second blessing." The whole bit.

The heavy diet on the Holy Spirit worked on everybody else, but I had trouble with it. When I started thinking for myself, I chose the old Calvinist tradition. Logical. Intellectual. And safe.

In seminary, when some of my friends "got involved" in the charismatic movement, I went the other way. Secure in my own theological bunker, I was not about to give over the control of my life to some mystical power.

### There's Gotta Be Something More

Twenty-five years later, I have come full circle . . . almost. I am rereading the Christian mystics who talk about intimacy with God: Andrew Murray's *Abide in Christ,* Hannah Whitall Smith's *The Christian's Secret of a Happy Life,* William Law's *A Serious Call to a Devout and Holy Life,* and Hudson Taylor's *Union and Communion.*

A few of my charismatic friends still "push my button" when they insist on my having their experience, but I cannot live off the dehydrated diet of powdered words and frozen fellowship that seems to be the alternative.

Somehow, somewhere . . . there's got to be more to this Christian life. This is what this course is all about.

### Quadraphonic Living

In this course, you will see where I have been scratching. You will find the usual appetizers and hors d'oeuvres for building